EVE & the ETERNAL TREASURE

EMANUEL KAPLAN

Illustrated by

Mattias Fridh

To my parents.

ONCE UPON A TIME, there was a young girl named Eve. She decided one day to leave the house and have a walk. It was a lovely summer day - the wind was on a break, the clouds had somewhere else to be and the sun was standing high up in the sky, shining down on the lovely birds and the beautiful flowers. Eve walked down the green path towards the lake. Arriving at the lake, she saw how the sun was reflecting in the water. She also saw rings spreading out here and there. It was the fishes coming up having a quick sunbathe.

Eve sat down and looked out over the lake, took a deep breath and closed her eyes. She felt how the sun was warming her cheeks. She took another deep breath and listened to the birds, singing beautifully. She closed her eyes, it was calm and in that calmness she dozed off. It was like a dream…..

Eve stood up, and started walking, she arrived at a crooked path. For some reason, she couldn't recognise where she was anymore. She had walked this path several times before. It seemed like the world behind her had disappeared. She was still standing in nature and because it was a lovely day, she sighed and said loudly to herself:

"Well, might as well continue and see where I end up."

   After a while of walking, she got tired and out of nowhere, she saw a nice little
house. It had red walls, with a red roof and white windows. Smoke was coming out of
the chimney and the closer she came to the house, the more it smelled of freshly baked
cinnamon buns. She felt how the smell filled her with joy, energy and she sped up.
When Eve arrived at the house, she knocked on the small door.
   It felt like an eternity, before the door opened. An old lady with thick glasses, white
hair and a long cardigan over something that looked like a nightgown, stood there.
Eve looked at the old lady and smiled.

"I smelled the freshly baked cinnamon buns so I thought I'll knock on the door and see if I can help you with anything?"

The old lady looked at the girl, and smiled.

"You know what, I could need some help from someone young and strong like you. Would you please help me with the tray and put it on the table outside?"

Eve hurried inside, saw the tray with two glasses of cold milk and the most delicious cinnamon buns she had ever seen. She carried out the tray, walking slowly and carefully not to spill anything. Arriving at the table, they sat down and the old lady said to her with a smile.

"Help yourself, enjoy!"

Eve ate, and it tasted heavenly, took a big bite and swallowed it with a glass of milk. When she was finished she asked the old lady.

"What's your name?"

"My name is Veronica, and yours?"

"I am Eve."

Eve smiled as she sank into the cozy chair and began to doze off. The birds sang and it reminded her of the lake, near by her house. Veronica saw that Eve was comfortable and thought she would speak with her.

"How do you like my baking and the surroundings?"

Eve looked at Veronica.

"I like it here. It is nice, cozy and I wouldn't want to be anywhere else."

Veronica giggled.

"Well Eve, if you stay where it is nice and cozy, you won't be able to go on the adventure and find the treasure."

"I don't want to go anywhere. I like it here, exactly where I am!"

Eve, realized her heartbeat was increasing and she was taking shorter breaths. Why on earth would she leave her lovely place at home? She thought.

"Wait a minute, what treasure are you talking about?"

"Let me explain Eve. It's nice, safe and sound here, exactly where you are. However, everyone will make at least one journey in their lifetime. It could be that you go to a different place or it could also mean that you travel within yourself, like an inner journey. These two usually go together, but they don't need to." Veronica answered.

"Imagine the largest green meadow you've ever seen. On this meadow there are a lot of hills, some are high and others are low. On the other side of the meadow, is the treasure with everything you desire. When you start walking towards the treasure, you will encounter the hills. If you by any chance encounter a hill that is so high, you can't even see the top, then it is important that you take one step at a time and focus on the top, even though you can't see it. You don't need to move fast as long as you are moving forward, because reaching great heights can take some time. As long as you are patient, you'll be fine."

Eve looked suspiciously at Veronica and asked:

"Does the treasure really exist? What is the treasure if it exists? You aren't trying to trick me?

"No Eve, I would never do that. The treasure has everything you need."

Eve raised her eyebrows.

"How do I find the treasure? What do I need to do?"

"You'll get to learn it on the way there. When you leave my house, walk straight ahead and where the path splits, you'll find a sign with direction either back to your home or a sign with the text "Treasure". When you decide to take the "Treasure" road, you'll come to all the hills I've been talking about."

Veronica smiled and winked with her left eye.

"My friends live by the road. You might meet them if you choose to walk down that path.

They are a bit special, in their own way, just like you and I are special. If you want, they could help you."

There was something with how Veronica spoke and with the warm air around Eve that made her believe that the treasure might really exist, for real. She jumped up from the chair and looked at Veronica.

"Thank you very much Veronica! I must hurry, the sooner I start the sooner I'll get to the treasure."

"Wait, have a cinnamon bun with you on the road, if you get hungry."

Eve had already left, it was as if the wind had swooped her away and she was too excited to even think about something to eat.

Time passed by and when Eve had walked uphill and downhill on as many hills that she could count, she saw at a distance a young boy, young like her and it seemed like he was hoovering in the air. She approached, and could see that he was lying on a big stone and it was the high grass that covered it.

"Hello. HELLO!" Eve screamed to get the young boy's attention.

The hoovering young boy, looking a couple of years older than Eve, woke up
with a snoring.

"What? What happened?"
He rubbed the sleep out of his eyes and looked at Eve in front of him.
"Well hello, what are you doing here?" He said with a big smile.

Eve looked around. The boy was radiating the same kindness and warmth that she
had felt from Veronica.

"Where is the treasure?"

"What treasure?"

"The treasure Veronica was talking about."

"Aha! I see, so you have just been at Veronica's, had she baked those lovely
cinnamon buns? Did you get to eat them with a glass of milk? They are so lovely. I love
it when she bakes them and invites me over."

"Yes I did and it was delicious."

"Welcome my friend, my name is Freddie. A friend of Veronica is a friend of mine.
How may I help you? But first, what is your name?"

Eve was already impatient and frustrated with all the questions that didn't have to
do with the treasure.

"I am Eve! Show me the treasure! Where is it? The treasure Veronica was
talking about."

"Oh, you mean THAT treasure? I am sorry, I can't help you, because I don't know
what kind of treasure you are looking for."

Freddie tilted his head and looked deep into Eve's eyes.

Eve clenched her fists, stamped with her foot and snorted. She was irritated at
Veronica, because she had told her that Freddie would help her on the journey to find
the treasure, but now he was only asking questions.

"Hey come on! Let's play a game, what do you say?" Freddie said.

He smiled from ear to ear and his eyes were filled with joy. Eve couldn't be upset when she looked into his friendly eyes. The worst of her anger had left her.

"What kind of game?"

"A game where we imagine, and act like other people, a game I call the acting game."

"How are we supposed to do that Freddie?"

"We imagine and act like the person we would like to be. When we do that, we can feel, think and hear whatever the person would do. I call it, go into character. Look here Eve, I can see that you are upset with what Veronica told you. However if we play that you are Veronica, you might get some kind of clue about what she actually meant. What do you say?"

"But how am I supposed to know what she thinks, see what she sees, hear what she hears and feel what she feels? What kind of nonsense is this? I don't have time for this. Who could possibly be able to do this kind of thing?"

Freddie looked at her and smiled.

"Have faith and trust, especially in yourself that whatever you encounter, you can handle it. You already have everything you need within you."

Eve became even more skeptical. She couldn't grasp what he was talking about, even though he was kind and warm.

"There you see a tree and next to the tree, a couple of steps away, is a rock that is a little bit bigger than you and me. The tree and the rock are the characters on stage. When you stand next to the tree you will act as Veronica, when you stand by the rock you will act as Eve, and when you stand here with me, we will be the audience looking at the play and talking about what's going on. Everything will be done one step at a time.

Eve shrugged her shoulders and moved closer to Fred.

"Go and stand next to the rock. When you stand next to the rock you are acting as yourself, remember?"

"What do you mean to act as myself? I am Eve!"

"I apologize, I mean just be yourself and ask your questions to Veronica." Freddie corrected himself with a nervous smile.

"I can't see Veronica, what are you talking about? I can only see that old tree."

Fred took a deep breath and sighed.

"Yes I know. Come on, play along and use your imagination. Imagine that the tree is Veronica and what would you like to ask her?"

Eve prepared herself and looked at the tree:

"Where is the treasure? I walked the "Treasure" road, now I am with Freddie and he is getting on my nerves."

"See, that wasn't that hard? Now let's move over to the tree."

Eve moved over with heavy steps, thinking this wasn't helping her at all.

"Well, now what? I am standing here and where is Veronica?"

Fred giggled and thought loudly.

"Everytime it is the same."

He looked at her with his warm eyes.

"Just feel, don't think Eve! Feel being Veronica, see her in front of you, and hear her voice. What do you think she would have said, if she spoke to you right here, right now? What I am trying to say is, act as if you are Veronica."

Eve closed her eyes, took a deep breath, focused and in the same moment she was filled with an energy and a force that she'd never felt before. She stood like Veronica, talked like her and moved like her, it was as if Eve could see, feel and hear what Veronica would have percieved in that specific moment. Then it was over.

Eve felt like she went back to being herself. The powerful energy had aligned and was balanced with hers. She couldn't make sense of any that had happened. When she opened her eyes, she saw Freddie's warm smile.

"Come, stand next to me here."

He stood a couple of steps aways from the tree and the rock.

"You and I will now be the audience witnessing what just happened on the imaginary stage. We'll look at it from where we are standing right now. What did you think happened? What have you learned from this?"

Eve looked at the old tree and the rock that was a bit bigger than her and Fred.

"I don't know, I just feel like a failure because I haven't found the treasure."

"Don't say that Eve! You know what? There are no failures, only mistakes, and we all make mistakes. It's part of life, if we don't dare to make any mistakes, we won't be learning anything either. It is by making mistakes, learning from them and moving on with what you've learned, that you discover the world. It is up to you and each and every one of us, to choose how we would like to relate to our mistakes. If it is something we use to help us move on, or if we let it be something that holds us back. Look at the old tree and the rock on our imaginary stage, feel what you feel, see what you see, hear what you hear and tell me, what you as a spectator have learned from the play we just saw?"

Eve stood there, her mind was working like a saw going through a big oak tree.

"Speak your thoughts so I can hear what you are thinking," said Fred.

Eve took a deep breath and prepared herself.

"I don't know. I have no idea. I did my best but nothing happened." She stood there shrugging her shoulders.

Freddie smiled.

"Eve, sometimes even though we do our best, there is no guarantee that we'll succeed. I can promise you that if you always do your best, you will always learn something new. It could also lead to doors you never knew existed, opening for you."

Freddie took out something from his pocket, it looked like a piece of paper
and while unfolding it he said to Eve.

"While you were on your way here, Veronica sent me a message."

He started reading.

"I see you have reached Freddie. He is a boy with a great sense of humor, and I can see that he is encouraging you to play the acting game too. He wants to guide you so that you can find the answers yourself, even though it might feel a bit odd. The treasure you are looking for is close, yet far away. Only a few lucky ones find it. Those who do don't have any hunger for anything else and don't need anything else. If you want to find it, you will need to continue your journey over the hills to meet the third person. He may or may not confuse you, it depends on how you perceive it. It might seem that he speaks in a strange way, however, he has a purpose for doing it, and that is because he's speaking directly to your heart.

If you choose to continue to find the third person, you might lose your courage and your faith. When you are in your weakest moment, look up into the sky, you'll see one of the clouds resembling an anchor. At that moment, sit up, close your eyes, take a couple of deep breaths, and relax. Imagine that you are sitting by a campfire close to the lake by your home. Just breathe and imagine that the fire is warming your heart and filling you with energy. After doing this, you'll have the courage and energy to continue to find the third person."

He looked at Eve, smiling, while holding the piece of paper with both hands.

"One more thing, Eve. Sometimes, when you do your best and truly believe in it deep down in your heart, you may receive some unexpected help along the way."

He paused and let what he said sink in for a moment.

What do you say, Eve? Would you like to continue your journey even though you don't know if you'll find the treasure?"

Eve felt her spirit rise. She had done her best, didn't get what she wanted, but she got a clue instead, that could help her in her journey. She thought and decided that she liked the journey.

"Yes of course! If I return now, I'll never find the treasure."

"I am glad that you have decided to move on, you will learn a lot from the third. The sooner you get going, the sooner you'll find him."

Eve thanked Fred and went on her way.

She came to a new meadow, it stretched out like a vast green ocean.
The further she looked, the more it seemed the greenery melded with the distant
blue sky at the horizon. The hills looked even higher. With each step, she got more
tired, as if time itself had slowed. Little by little her strong will faded, remembering
the warnings Veronica had mentioned in her letter. Eventually, Eve's legs gave up, her
heart beating in protest. Falling onto the grass, the temptation to go back to her cozy
little house by the lake, where she could lose herself in the melody of bird song for
hours, pulled at her fiercely.

"If only I'd stayed home." She said to herself.

Eve rolled over onto her back. The first thing she noticed in the blue sky was a cloud shaped like an anchor. Her heart jumped, giving her new energy and removing the worst of her tiredness. She smiled, remembering Veronica's words from her letter about seeing a cloud looking like an anchor. Eve sat up, closed her eyes, and imagined herself by the lakeside campfire near her home. Imagining the flames warming her and filling her heart with energy, she took a few deep breaths before opening her eyes again.

"Wow! Veronica was telling the truth!" She cried out.

All her fatigue, despair, and uncertainty vanished. With renewed courage, increased energy, and determination, Eve continued on with her journey, singing her favorite song. Though unsure of the exact direction to take, she felt butterflies in her stomach, a sensation that moved her onward.

Time passed and when she reached another crossroad, she stopped to catch her breath. At this point, she didn't have any idea on which way she had to choose. When Eve was standing there and thinking, a giant smoke cloud appeared out of nowhere. She heard someone cough in the smoke cloud and then someone came speeding through in a wheelchair. It was a wheelchair that could go by itself and it stopped right in front of her. The person sitting in the chair had nice black and gray striped hair. He was well dressed, wearing a blazer, a white shirt, a bow tie and his nice hair was combed in a regular haircut.

"Hey there, what brings you here looking all that flare?" the man smiled at Eve.

She glanced at his outfit, his seat, and his hair. When their eyes locked, it felt as though time stood still. The silence was so profound that she could hear a pin drop. Unsure of what to say, she found herself uttering.

"I have met Veronica and Fred, they both told me that I would meet you and that you would help me find the treasure."

"Oh, really now, you don't say? Fred and Veronica, my friends, any day?"

Eve felt that she had come back to herself, she could feel the wind again. The man in front of her smelled of good perfume and he spoke in a strange way.

"Are you going to help me find the treasure or not?"

The man gave her half a smile.

"The treasure you seek may not be near, my dear. Should you search or let it be? It's not quite clear. Some say without it, peace won't be near. Take your time, listen, don't fear. Connected to you, the journey may appear slow, but color needn't disappear. It's you who'll find it, with a joyful cheer."

The words danced around in Eve's head, and disappeared, as if he never had spoken. Her heart pounded harder, she tied her fists and bit her jaws. Eve spoke through her teeth.

"I have no idea what you are saying! Just answer my question like ordinary people, please!"

"Who are ordinary people? Could they be the common crowd? Or anyone, proud?"

"Everyone!" answered Eve.

"Who's everyone? Could it be anyone? Or maybe you, my dear one?" The old man's eyebrows shot up, revealing his surprise.

"Allright, would you please talk like Veronica and Fred? If you are friends, you should know."

"Aha, so that's what's on your mind, standing there, patient, eyes blinking so kind. Well then, Eve, you needn't deceive. Though you've walked valleys, faced hardship in rows, reaching the finale, no more dillydally, yet still, what you seek, it seems to elude. Or perhaps, it's time to awaken, no more sleep, to find the treasure within, so deep, a secret to keep, yours to pursue. For you see, dear, it's been there all along, not in the valleys, not in the throngs, but in your heart's song. As sure as my name's Mike, that much is true."

POFF! In the same moment the man had said his name he vanished. Eve got lift up in the air. It became darker around her, she was hoovering and traveled far away through the galaxy. She saw all the stars shining with their light, to then just turn into lines as she moved faster and faster. Eve went into a dark tunnel, it became narrower and finally it went pitch black. No sight, no sound and no presence of anything.

Eve opened her eyes and the first thing she saw was the blue sky. She jumped up, feeling lighter than ever. She looked around and realized that she had fallen asleep by the lake. Eve glanced out at the lake and noticed something glowing being reflected in the water. As she drew nearer, the glow grew stronger and more intense. Peering down at the water, she saw her own image surrounded by the most dazzling glow she had ever seen. It was breathtaking, yet strangely familiar.

Eve picked up a small rock and tossed it into the lake. To her surprise, it skipped farther than any rock she had ever thrown. Looking at her hands, she felt a sense of power and strength flowing through her. It felt as though everything had aligned perfectly. The trees appeared even more beautiful, the grass felt softer, and the birds sang more sweetly. Her heart beat with a newfound sense of joy. With light and springy steps, a smile gracing her lips, she continued her walk. For in that moment, she knew she had discovered the treasure within herself.

— THE END —

www.emanuelkaplan.com